There are millions (OK, thousands) of books about diet and eating. Most do their best to make these simple subjects complicated. We reckon we can tell you all you need to know in 36 easy-to-read pages.

Would you like to:

> Feel better?

> Look better?

> Gain energy?

> Avoid that mid-afternoon slump?

> Wake up refreshed?

> Gain muscle?

> Lose a bit of flab?

> Lower your blood pressure?

> Lower your cholesterol?

> Improve your blood sugar levels?

> Enjoy a better sex life?

The fuel you put in your tank can make a big difference to all of them.

WHEN TO EAT

This guide is mainly about what to eat but when you eat is just as important.

Breakfast is the most important meal of the day. Having gone without fuel overnight, you need to fill the empty tank. If you don't, your body goes into emergency mode, breaking down muscle to burn. Then, because you're hungry, you eat more than you need later in the day, perhaps grabbing less healthy snacks because they're quick and easy.

Either three 'square' meals a day or more frequent, smaller meals are fine. It's all about not consuming more energy than you need.

It is important to maintain blood sugar levels and regular snacks can help. Grazing need not lead to higher weight if you choose the right things. But, if you are overweight, think about how you snack: obese men tend to eat more snacks more often and tend to eat more cakes, biscuits, sweets, chocolate and desserts. Not rocket science, is it?

For healthier snack choices, see Snack Attack on page 28.

CONTENTS

Text by Dr Sarah Brewer • Edited by Jim Pollard
Cartoons by John Byrne • Advisory Board: John Chisholm, Richard Miller,
Frankie Phillips, Dr Judy Swift (University of Nottingham) • Images: MHF and
creativecommons.org (Credits p35) • Supported by Danio
Published: February 2015 • Revision date: February 2017.

TWO-THIRDS OF UK MEN ARE OVERWEIGHT OR OBESE...

3 8002 02314 145 2

FOOD IS GREAT. ENJOY IT.

Every cell in your body is made up from what you eat and drink, what you breathe and very little else.

This booklet is about enjoying a wide range of tasty foods in a flexible, hassle-free way, whether eating in or out. You'll get all the energy, protein, essential fatty acids, vitamins and minerals you need for good health – including the fibre and fluids to keep your bowels in tip-top order (you know what we mean).

Eating well helps you to:

> maintain a healthy weight

> avoid high blood pressure or raised cholesterol

> stay clear of type 2 diabetes, heart disease, stroke and even some cancers.

It's easier than you think. Even little changes will help. Read on.

EATING WELL WILL HELP YOU TO:

> **EXERCISE BETTER**   > **CONCENTRATE MORE**

> **WORK MORE EFFICIENTLY**   > **FEEL MORE POSITIVE**

IT CAN EVEN IMPROVE YOUR RELATIONSHIPS AND SEX LIFE
                                          (REALLY!)

SLOW DOWN!

Do you wolf down meals to get on with more important things in life?

By eating more slowly you'll enjoy your food more, eat less and make healthier choices. (Thinking about what we've already eaten also helps us make healthier choices.) Sit down at a table, even if on your own. It helps you appreciate your food and see how much you've eaten.

Distractions like TV, phone surfing or reading can mean you eat more without realising - yet feel less satisfied by your meal.

Notice what you're eating and how it tastes. **Chew more slowly** and thoroughly.

Try putting your fork down between mouthfuls, using smaller cutlery, eating with your non-dominant hand (left if you normally hold your spoon in the right) or even eating with chopsticks to slow things down.

Really? Yes, research shows mindfulness - or being aware of what you're doing and feeling in the moment that you're doing and feeling it - reduces stress and blood pressure and helps digestion and weight loss.

CHEW ON IT

Two groups of men were asked to chew each mouthful of pizza either 15 or 40 times before swallowing. Three hours later, those who chewed 40 times were much less hungry and less interested in eating. Their blood sugar and hormone levels suggested that chewing more may make you feel fuller and improve the way your body absorbs nutrients.

SKIPPING BREAKFAST KILLS

A 16-year study, involving almost 27,000 men, found those who skipped breakfast were more likely to have a fatal heart attack than those who didn't.

Why? Because skipping breakfast increased their risk of obesity, high blood pressure, high cholesterol and diabetes.

TAKING TIME OVER YOUR MEALS IS HEALTHIER...

THAT'S NO EXCUSE FOR TAKING TWO HOURS TO SERVE ME!

EAT BETTER EXERCISE BETTER

When you eat well, you can exercise harder, for longer, and recover more quickly.

During exercise, the rate at which your muscles burn energy increases by as much as 20 times, so exercising muscle needs a quick source of energy: glucose (sugar). Some comes from the starchy glycogen (stored sugar) in your muscles, but most comes from your circulation. This is why regular exercise lowers your risk of type 2 diabetes. To fuel your muscles:

> **Try complex carbohydrates** (eg wholegrain bread, brown rice, wholemeal pasta, wholemeal crispbread, wholegrain cereals such as shredded wheat, weetabix, porridge or unsweetened muesli)

> **Eat more starchy vegetables**, including peas, beans, lentils and sweet potatoes

> **Eat fruit as snacks** - bananas are good as they are portable and help replenish your body's carbohydrate stores after exercise. (Whole fruit, not smoothies.)

Light exercise such as walking off a meal reduces the rise in blood sugar and fat levels that can lead to weight gain, hardening of the arteries, raised blood pressure and cholesterol and type 2 diabetes. Watch out for cramp or heartburn though.

For general health, two and a half hours (150 minutes) of moderate exercise (or 75 minutes of vigorous exercise) a week is recommended. If you also want to lose weight, you should be active for an additional 60 minutes, at least three times a week.

DRINK WATER FIRST

Although sweat contains dissolved salts (electrolytes), you lose much more water than salt during intense exercise. You need to replace this fluid loss by drinking at least a pint of plain, tap or bottled water before you start drinking electrolyte solutions or those containing glucose.

WHAT ABOUT SPORTS DRINKS?

For most men, the best fluid to drink before and during exercise is either plain water or natural coconut water (for a bit of flavour). Dilute (hypotonic) sports drinks may have a place if you are working-out but are not needed if you are exercising for less than an hour. Anyway, diluted fruit juice or squash work just as well.

Hypotonic Drinks contain a lower concentration of salts than body fluids plus 2 to 3 grams sugar per 100ml. These are best consumed after a general workout to top up muscle energy stores.

Isotonic Drinks contain the same concentration of salts as body fluids plus 6 to 7 grams sugar per 100ml, so provide more energy. These are designed for professional athletes such as middle- and long-distance runners and those doing team sports.

IT'S THE LATEST SPORTS DRINK- TASTES LIKE OLD RUGBY SOCKS!

Carbohydrate or Energy (hypertonic) Drinks contain even higher quantities of dissolved salts and 10 to 20 grams of sugar per 100ml. They are only useful to replenish your carbohydrate stores if your exercise session extends beyond the 60-minute mark or if you are an athlete who requires energy without fluid (eg. gymnast, weight lifter).

DON'T USE ENERGY DRINKS IF YOU DON'T NEED TO

Don't use energy drinks when you don't need them. If you haven't been exercising for at least an hour, they supply unneeded sugar and calories like any other unneeded snack.

What's more, the sugar in energy drinks and sweetened, acidic or fizzy beverages can damage your teeth. Using a straw positioned towards the back of your mouth reduces the contact time between your teeth and the drink and may reduce the damage.

Mixing alcohol with energy drinks increases the risk of alcohol poisoning because the caffeine keeps you going so you drink more. Energy drinks also create a 'wired' feeling which, when combined with alcohol, may lead you to do things that you wouldn't usually want to.

ONLY SERIOUS ATHLETES NEED CAFFEINE

Performance-enhancing high-energy drinks may contain high amounts of caffeine. These have been linked to serious side effects such as heart palpitations, caffeine intoxication and even death. They are best avoided if you are not exercising vigorously.

However, for a serious athlete, consuming the equivalent of 3-4mg of caffeine per kilogram of bodyweight (so 210-280 mg for someone weighing 70kg) one hour before exercise has been shown to improve endurance and performance in a variety of sports, including cycling, high-intensity running, repeated sprinting, football and rugby. The effects last 80 to 90 minutes.

EAT BETTER FEEL BETTER

Studies show we are more likely to eat junk when in a bad mood, but find it easier to make healthy choices when happy. This cuts both ways. In other words, if you eat healthily, you're more likely to feel happy and cope better with stress.

The chemicals in healthy foods, and the feelings of enjoyable eating influence your mood and impulses: you make better decisions without realising. They can also improve your sleep.

Fish, for example, contains omega-3 fatty acids which boost emotional well-being. A so-called Mediterranean-style diet (which is based on vegetables, fruits, whole grains, fish and beans) is also linked with a more positive mood, especially as you get older.

BEAT STRESS AND PREVENT MOOD SWINGS

The way different foods containing carbohydrates (carbs) affect blood sugar level is known as their glycaemic index (GI). Foods that rapidly increase blood sugar have a high GI; foods that have little impact on blood sugar have a low GI.

Eating foods with a high GI may feel like a good idea when you're stressed out and drained of energy, but it's not. A rise in sugar levels triggers the release of insulin, the hormone which pushes sugar out of your blood stream into your cells. If you eat high GI, the effects of insulin may cause a downfall in blood sugar levels a few hours later, leaving you feeling even more drained.

As your brain cells need more sugar than other tissue, this low blood sugar reduces your ability to concentrate and think straight. In other words, you may feel calm two hours after eating a higher GI (carbohydrate-rich) meal but this may well be followed by a post-meal slump so you are less able to pay attention – this is even more noticeable as you get older.

So, when you're feeling stressed, go easy on foods with a high GI and select foods with a low to moderate GI. Combining small amounts of food with a high GI (eg mashed potatoes) with those of lower GI (eg beans) also helps prevent up and down swings in blood sugar levels.

HIGH GI > GO EASY

Parsnips, baked potatoes, cornflakes, raisins, donuts, bread, mashed potatoes, dried fruit.

MEDIUM GI > EAT MODERATELY

White rice, honey, boiled new potatoes, fresh apricots, bananas, potato chips, sweetcorn, porridge oats, muesli.

LOW GI > EAT MORE FREELY (BUT DON'T GO MAD!)

Carrots, lettuce, tomato, cucumber, peppers, small portion brown rice, mango, Kiwi fruit, unsweetened bran cereal, peas, grapes, sweet potato, baked beans, small portion wholewheat pasta (cooked al dente), orange, apple, pears.

THINK ABOUT YOUR GI, JOE

The overall GI of a meal depends on the combination of foods you select and portion sizes. Take a food with a high GI (eg a baked potato). Combine it with a protein source (eg skinned chicken breast). Add a large mixed salad. Result: a healthy, balanced meal. This way of eating is particularly helpful for people with diabetes. For more on the glycaemic index, visit www.nhs.uk.

HOW TO FILL YOUR PLATE

Fill **HALF** your plate with salad or vegetables, one **QUARTER** with protein (eg lean meat, fish, eggs, beans) and one **QUARTER** with starchy carbs (eg brown rice, wholewheat pasta, quinoa, baked potato, noodles). Try a smaller plate. You might be surprised it fills you up and you can still 'go big' on green vegetables and salads.

START THE DAY RIGHT

Levels of the stress hormone, cortisol, are highest in the morning due to the physical 'stress' of your overnight fast. Eating a nutritious breakfast is especially important.

SNAPPY SHOPPER

Don't shop for food when hungry or fed up. You are less likely to make healthy choices. So, if shopping after work (when you might be feeling both), be aware. Perhaps have a banana or apple as a pre-shopping snack.

EAT BETTER
HAVE BETTER SEX

A lot of rubbish is written on this topic but some basic food ingredients may help improve your sexual energy, testosterone levels, fertility and staying power.

It's all about getting the right amounts of the vitamins and minerals which play a key role in reproduction and libido. Lack of zinc, for example, lowers testosterone levels. As you lose between 1mg and 3mg zinc per ejaculation, eating some zinc-rich foods is a must.

Casanova ate oysters to boost his libido. As well as a rich source of zinc, oysters contain rare amino acids (protein-building blocks) that increase your level of sex hormones.

This table shows which vitamins and minerals are important for your sex drive and where to find them. Get your 5-a-day fruit and veg, regular weekly portions of seafood and a daily handful of unsalted nuts and you won't go far wrong.

Sexual Function	Nutrients	Food sources
Healthy testosterone levels and sex drive	Vitamin A	Animal and fish livers, kidneys, eggs, milk, cheese, yoghurt, butter, oily fish, meat, margarine, dark green leafy vegetables and yellow-orange fruits
	Magnesium	Soya beans, nuts, yeast, wholegrains, brown rice, seafood, meat, eggs, dairy products, bananas, green leafy vegetables, dark chocolate, cocoa
	Zinc	Red meat (especially offal), seafood (especially oysters), yeast, wholegrains, pulses, eggs, cheese
Healthy Sperm	Vitamin C	All fruit and veg, especially citrus, blackcurrants, guavas, Kiwi fruit, peppers, strawberries, green sprouting vegetables
	Vitamin E	Oily fish, fortified margarine and dairy products, liver, eggs
	Selenium	Brazil nuts (the richest source), other tree nuts, broccoli, mushrooms, cabbage, radishes, onions, garlic, celery, wholegrains, yeast, seafood, offal
Stamina and staying power	B vitamins	Yeast extracts, brown rice, wholegrain bread and cereals, seafood, poultry and meat (especially offal), pulses, nuts, eggs, dairy products, green leafy vegetables
	Iron	Red meat (especially offal), seafood, wheatgerm, wholemeal bread, egg yolk, green vegetables, prunes and other dried fruit
	Iodine	Seafood, seaweed, iodised salt
Arousal and orgasm	Calcium	Milk, yoghurt, cheese, green vegetables, oranges, bread
	Phosphorus	Dairy products, yeast, soya beans, nuts, wholegrains, eggs, poultry, meat and fish.

WHY COUPLES FIGHT

Food – or lack of it - can also affect how you or your partner responds to amorous advances.

Research suggests that hunger related to low blood sugar levels is a major cause of domestic arguments, regardless of the overall quality of your relationship.

LOW BLOOD SUGAR TRIGGERS ANGER

Low blood sugar triggers anger and aggression because glucose is the major fuel for brain cells, and the energy needed to control aggressive impulses is less available when blood glucose is low.

The best thing to avoid being a 'hangry' partner is to avoid skipping meals.

FOOD FAQS

With a few exceptions, there are no good and bad foods. It's about quantity and balance.

For some of us, getting the right balance may just mean cutting back on portion sizes.

For others, it may mean replacing habits that make us feel worse (such as skipping meals and avoiding fruit or veg) with ones that make us feel better (such as eating breakfast and snacking on fruit rather than biscuits).

Your cells need energy to work properly. This energy (measured in calories) comes from the carbs, protein, fat and alcohol in your diet.

WHAT ARE THE BEST CEREALS TO EAT?

Go for unsweetened wholegrain cereals such as unsugared muesli, shredded wheat, weetabix or oatmeal porridge. (Granola too is full of good stuff but high in calories.) Want to cut down on sugar? Changing cereal could be the way.

Serve with semi-skimmed milk, unsweetened yoghurt/fromage frais or dairy-free alternative such as soy, almond, rice or oat milks. Look for milk alternatives that are calcium-enriched. Add fresh berries, nuts or chopped fruit for extra flavour.

WHAT CAUSES A BEER GUT?

Calories and the way men store fat around their bellies. It's not just alcohol. Sugary drinks can do the same. Alcohol and sugar contain stacks of calories and are often consumed when you are not hungry and so don't need them.

Alcohol is 7 calories per gram, compared to around 4 calories per gram for carbohydrates, such as sugar, and proteins such as those found in lean meat and beans. Only fats and oils are more energy-dense than alcohol at 9 calories of energy per gram.

IS SUGAR ADDICTIVE?

Carbohydrates affect mood by triggering the release of feel-good brain chemicals such as serotonin. This can make you crave similar foods but these effects are not as addictive as nicotine or, for some people, alcohol. The craving we often have after a meal for something sweet will pass.

Scientists have also found stress hormone receptors within the taste buds that detect sweetness which may explain why we turn to sweet foods when stressed.

If you crave something sweet, distract yourself. Exercise will do this best - a walk or run - as it will burn off the effects of stress and also curb the cravings - but anything that keeps you absorbed will help. If you can't get away, drink water or herbal tea.

HOW DO YOU READ FOOD LABELS?

With difficulty sometimes. But you can learn to speak the lingo.

Most pre-packed foods have a nutrition label on the packaging which tells you how much energy, protein, carbohydrate and fat they contain (per 100g and often per serving, too). They may also show information on saturated fat, sugars, sodium and salt.

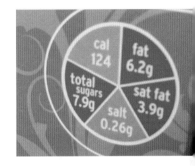

Ingredients are listed in order of quantity.

If sugar is one of the first words on a list, it may contain more than is good for you. Similarly, if there's a lot of E numbers and words that sound more like chemicals than foods, you may want to steer clear.

The Red, Amber and Green traffic-light flashes show how a particular food or drink fits into your daily diet.

In general, the more green on the label, the healthier it's likely to be.

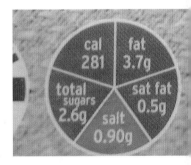

Red on the label means the product is high in saturated fat, salt or sugars and these are the foods most of us need to cut back on. So, if you pick up two similar products, the label should help you select the healthier option. That's the theory, anyway.

SO HOW MUCH SUGAR?

Free sugar should be no more than **5%** of your daily calories (but aim lower.)

Free sugar is essentially the sugars you have some control over. It includes sugar in manufactured or processed food plus sugar or honey you add to food but excludes sugar found naturally in fruit, veg and dairy. So sugar in an apple doesn't count but sugar in apple juice does (since juice is processed).

Five percent is about 30g of free sugar a day (the equivalent of just seven sugar cubes) so check labels and go very easy on sugar you add yourself.

SHOULD I ADD SALT TO FOOD?

No. Some of us cannot process excess salt (sodium chloride) through our kidneys, leading to a rise in blood pressure.

Aim to eat less than 6g salt per day, which for most men means cutting back. Go easy with salted nuts, crisps, soy sauce and meat or vegetable extract spreads and instead of adding salt to meals, try black pepper, herbs and/or garlic. Or a little low-sodium salt.

HIGH SALT?

A lot of salt is hidden in processed foods, so check labels:

0.3g (per 100g) of salt or less is a **LITTLE** salt

1.5g (per 100g) of salt or more is a **LOT** of salt.

ARE THERE REALLY 'GOOD' AND 'BAD' FATS?

The only really bad fats are **trans-fats** – fats artificially processed with water to make them spreadable. They are linked with health problems such as heart disease so manufacturers have begun to remove most of them from processed foods and spreads. But they're not actually illegal so avoid products that list partially-hydrogenated fat or oil on the label.

Some **saturated (animal) fats** are converted into cholesterol in the body. For this reason they were considered 'bad'. However, they are often present with good nutrients that minimise these effects (for example, egg yolks are also rich in lecithin and vitamins).

Monounsaturated fats (found, for example, in olive oil, nuts and avocados) and omega-3 fats (found, for example, in oily fish, rapeseed oil and walnuts) are called 'good' fats as they have beneficial effects on cholesterol balance in the body.

Remember though that **all fats are concentrated sources of energy** (9 calories per gram) so go easy. A little bit of everything does you good (except trans-fats). Use rapeseed or olive oil to cook with and extra virgin olive oil or nut oils for salad dressings. (But it's best not to cook with extra virgin olive oil as it smokes at lower temperatures and loses its benefits. Use plain olive oil.)

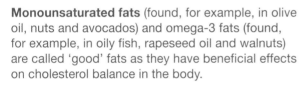

HIGH FAT?

When checking labels:

3g (per 100g - or per serving if less than 100g) is a **LITTLE** fat

17.5g (per 100g) is a **LOT** of fat

1.5g of **SATURATED** fat is a **LITTLE** fat

5g of **SATURATED** fat is a **LOT** of fat.

MEAT AND FISH

CAN I EAT MEAT?

Yes. Meat is an excellent source of protein, energy, vitamins and minerals (especially iron and zinc) but eating too much processed or char-grilled meat appears to increase the risk of bowel cancer.

Guidelines suggest no more than 90g red meat or processed meats such as bacon, sausages, ham or salami per day: **90g is around three thin slices of roast beef, lamb or pork.** Replacing half the meat in a recipe with chopped fresh mushrooms is an easy way to cut back on meat while adding flavour and filling power.

If you want to eat less meat, maintain your protein intake from pulses, soy products and Quorn (derived from a nutritious type of fungus and tastier than it sounds).

ANY EASY WAYS TO EAT FISH?

Yes. Plain tinned and prepared frozen fish are just as good as fresh and are easy to use in cooked dishes (tinned mackerel in a pasta sauce, for example) or sandwiches.

For fresh fish, fishmongers will do all the fiddly bits like removing skin and bones.

The simplest way to cook fresh fish is to brush with olive oil, add some fresh stuff (herbs, lemon juice and garlic), and either grill, steam or wrap in foil and bake

(which reduces cooking smells). Steam or bake vegetables alongside the fish.

Keep deep-fried, battered fish as an occasional treat as it's high in fat and calories – especially if served with deep-fried chips.

FRUIT AND VEG

WHY DON'T I LIKE VEGETABLES?

You probably do. The problem is often over-cooking.

Try them lightly steamed, stir-fried or flashed on a barbecue. Try more exotic options. Heard of rainbow chard, butternut squash or romanesco? Buy what's in season - much cheaper and, if local, often fresher and tastier.

Sweet potato is an alternative to regular white potato - they're packed full of vitamin A - while vegetarian curries, Chinese and Thai meals are so tasty you won't miss the meat.

DOES A SMOOTHIE COUNT AS A PORTION OF FRUIT?

If you include a good amount of whole fresh or frozen fruit and vegetables, **a home-made smoothie can count as up to two of your 5-a-day.**

Use a variety of different fruits and vegetables (carrot and beetroot are especially good) and add a few leaves of spinach or kale, too. You won't taste the extra leaves but they add extra vitamins, fibre and colour.

Shop-bought smoothies may have hidden extras like flavourings and much less fruit. Check labels. They should tell you whether they count as a portion. (Go easy: smoothie and fruit juice sugars may be natural but they are still free sugars - see p19.)

PERSONALLY I FIND A BIG BREAKFAST TOO HARD TO SWALLOW FIRST THING IN THE MORNING..

HAVE YOU TRIED TAKING THE CEREAL OUT OF THE BOX BEFORE YOU EAT IT?

WHAT'S SO GOOD ABOUT NUTS AND PULSES?

They taste great and are an excellent easy source of protein, vitamins, minerals and, in the case of nuts, 'good' monounsaturated and omega-3 oils. Soy beans are also full of isoflavones which help hormone balance and may even reduce your risk of prostate cancer.

> Chuck an extra can of beans in your chilli

> sprinkle some nuts and seeds on your cereal or stir-fry

> add a handful of red lentils to your bolognese.

WHAT'S SO BAD ABOUT PROCESSED FOOD?

With most foods, the less processed it is, the better it is for us. You're looking for the nearest to fresh you can find.

This is not always as obvious as it looks. Fish tinned at sea and veg frozen when picked may well have more nutrients than an ageing fish and veg meal packaged on the deli section to look nice and fresh.

Processed foods usually have higher levels of fat, sugar and/or salt than home-cooked versions and less of the important nutrients found in freshly-prepared foods. But eating them occasionally is fine. Check labels to avoid those with high contents of fat, sugar and/or salt.

To make home-cooked meals more convenient, batch cook and freeze extra portions for when time is tight. This means you get a home-cooked dinner quicker than a take-away, cheaper and with more of the good stuff.

Really easy: a massive soup. Braise chopped onion in a little oil for five minutes. Add water and your favourite veg chopped up. Simmer until soft and zap it with the blender. Cream it with soya milk. Flavour with spices and/or garlic. Lasts days. Plenty of recipes online.

Home-made is best as shop-bought soups are often high in salt and sugar.

WHAT ABOUT MILK AND DAIRY?

Yes. Milk and dairy products like cheese and yoghurt form part of a healthy diet. They are great sources of protein, calcium and B vitamins - but go easy: they contain saturated fat. Try semi-skimmed or low-fat instead of full-fat.

IS FOOD INTOLERANCE REAL OR A FAD?

Yes, some people react badly to foods that others eat without problems.

Classic **food allergy** triggers an immediate, serious reaction such as swelling of the mouth, difficulty breathing or collapse.

But some people become intolerant to certain foods because they lack an enzyme needed to digest it. For example, insufficient production of the enzyme, lactase, can cause an **intolerance to lactose sugar** found in milk.

Other types of food intolerance are less well understood.

If you develop a reaction such as headache, loose bowels or eczema which you think may be due to a food intolerance, get medical or dietary advice as just cutting foods from your diet could mean you don't get all the vitamins and minerals you need. (For example, stopping dairy may mean you don't get the calcium essential for bone strength.)

ALAN'S ALWAYS SUFFERED FROM FOOD INTOLERANCE...

LAB

E NUMBERS GO BACK WHERE YOU CAME FROM!

SUPPLEMENTS?

DO I NEED VITAMINS, MINERALS OR OTHER EXTRAS?

If you eat at least 5 fruit and veg a day, regular intakes of nuts and seeds, plus beans, fish and wholegrains, then you should get all the vitamins and minerals you need.

If you skip meals, hate vegetables, eat little fish, avoid the sun (which helps to make vitamin D in your skin), eat processed microwaved meals, and know your diet is not as good as it could be, you may benefit from a daily vitamin and mineral supplement.

Avoid mega-doses. Look for supplements supplying around 100% of the recommended daily amounts (RDAs) - also known as Nutrient Reference Values (NRVs).

IS THERE A POINT IN ORGANIC OR NON-GM FOODS?

There's a debate about whether organic foods are better than non-organic.

A review in the British Journal of Nutrition looked at 343 studies. It concluded that organic fruit, vegetables and cereals provide 20 to 40 percent more antioxidants – the equivalent of eating two extra portions of fruit and vegetables a day - with no increase in calories. Pesticide residues were also 10 to 100 times lower in organic foods compared with those conventionally grown.

But it comes down to personal choice. Although organic foods may contain lower levels of agricultural chemicals, it is generally accepted that pesticide residues remaining in non-organic food are not harmful to human health.

BRING ON A SUBSTITUTE

Small changes in what you eat and the amount of exercise you take can make a surprising difference to how you feel.

The British Dietetic Association suggest some smart swaps which **add variety, provide more nutrients and save calories**. And they add up. If you're interested in weight-loss, just these six swaps could help you shed up to a pound of fat (3500 calories) a week, every week. No hassle.

Take off the menu:	Substitute:	SAVE: Fat	Calories
Fried bacon, egg, sausage, tomatoes & hash browns	Grilled bacon, sausage & tomatoes, poached egg, wholemeal toast	56g	463
	OR Wholegrain breakfast cereal, semi-skimmed milk, glass of unsweetened orange juice	68g	466
Standard BLT sandwich	BLT with reduced-fat mayo and lean bacon	25g	326
Steak pie and chips	Shepherd's pie and veg	22g	268
150g whole milk creamy yoghurt	Low-fat yoghurt (which can still taste creamy!)	5g	99
Half pint full-cream milk	Half pint semi-skimmed milk	6g	57

SNACK ATTACK?

If you don't increase your overall calorie intake, then eating little and often is not a bad policy as it helps keep your metabolism ticking over nicely. In other words, **there's no problem with snacking as such**.

The French have a 'goûter', a little snack late afternoon which means they eat a smaller evening meal - bread with plain chocolate or fruit is popular.

The problem comes when snacking between meals – especially when you're not hungry - leads to eating too much.

Even one small, daily snack that's surplus to requirements will show on your waistline. Two plain biscuits or a can of sugary drink or a bag of crisps each break time could each see you put on around half a stone (3-4kg) a year. In real money, this could add four or more inches to your waistline.

Save these for an occasional treat. There are plenty of feel-good alternatives: fruit (bananas and apples travel well), low-calorie drinks (water or tea), nuts (unsalted), baked rather than fried crisps or unsweetened yoghurt.

THIRSTY?

Check your snack attack isn't due to thirst - drink enough fluids to keep your urine a pale straw colour, not dark yellow or brown.

MAKE SMART SNACKING CHOICES

> Swap a **Danish pastry** for a cereal bar and save 165 kcals while gaining extra vitamins, minerals and fibre! (Check the label.)

> Swap a 34.5g bag of **crisps** for a 28g bag of reduced-fat crisps to save 55 kcals. (This may not seem like much, but do it three times and you've saved the same amount of calories as in a pint of 5% strength beer.)

> Swap a small carton of **fruit juice** for a glass of water and save 94 kcals as well as protecting your teeth.

> Swap a can of sugary **fizzy drink** for a diet version and save 135 kcals while also reducing potentially harmful blood sugar swings.

Smart snacking saves money too - a supermarket banana is 20p, a Danish at least a quid.

Beat a snack attack with physical activity – a brisk walk, a cycle ride, gardening, housework (vacuuming is good) or DIY. If you can't get out and exercise, drinking water or herbal tea will take the edge off.

No-one to exercise with? Team up with others in your area via sites such as www.cyclingbuddy.com or www.play4ateam.com

SNACK CHECK

Check labels. A snack is likely to represent a healthy option if, per 100g, it contains:

> less than **3g fat**

> less than **2g sugar**

> less than **0.25g salt**
(or less than 0.1g sodium)

A snack is best avoided if, per 100g, it contains:

> **20g** or more **fat**

> **10g** or more **sugar**

> **1.25g** or more **salt**
(or more than 0.5g sodium)

For snacks with values in-between, handle with care.

CHANGING LIFE CHANGING DIET

When life changes so can your diet. Here are some ideas on how to eat more of the good stuff in different life circumstances.

LEAVING HOME

When going to college or starting work, your diet is likely to change to whatever is offered in the canteen or local sandwich shop. Check our advice on labels and choices. Look for cook books offering quick, easy, cheap yet nutritious recipes – many are available, such as Good Food 101 Easy Student Dinners (BBC Digital).

SHIFT-WORKING

Working shifts disrupts your natural body clock so set up a structured eating pattern to fight fatigue. This may mean taking meals and snacks with you. Eat regular smaller meals (eg. a before-shift 'breakfast' and a mid-shift 'lunch break') with planned snacks in-between rather than constantly snacking throughout your shift. Stay as active as possible to stay alert.

MOVING IN TOGETHER

Once you move in with your partner, you are three times more likely to become overweight than if you continue living separately. Obviously this doesn't apply to all couples but take note that moving in together is a time to watch (and we don't mean the television). You have been warned.

PARENTHOOD

Eating together as a family can encourage solid eating habits in your kids. Research shows children who regularly eat meals with their parents are more likely to get their 5-a-day. The benefits are seen even when families only sit down to eat together a couple of times a week.

DIVORCE

Some studies show that men gain weight after a divorce, others that they lose it. Either way, at a time of emotional upheaval, it's vital to eat well. Exercise is a great way to burn off the effects of stress hormones. Ask friends or family for their easy, favourite recipes, and look for cook books designed for those cooking for one such as Good Food: Meals for One (BBC Digital).

COMMUTING

Men in their early 40s spend on average 67 minutes a day commuting to and from work – 81 minutes for those in London. Carry decent snacking options such as fruit and water (add a slice of lemon for flavour).

UNEMPLOYMENT

Losing your job dramatically changes the structure of your day. Use extra time for exercise, cooking, trying new dishes and eating better for less money. For cheap fruit and veg, use local markets and go to supermarkets at the end of the day.

GETTING OLDER

As your metabolism slows with age and the amount of muscle you carry decreases, it's easy to put on body fat. The information in this booklet becomes even more important.

WHAT ABOUT EATING OUT?

The same rules apply as when eating at home – it's about balance. A little of what you fancy is fine but not every day so a big meal out is OK if you balance it with what you eat at home the rest of the week. The more you eat out, the more you need to be aware.

MENU MASTER

Know your menus. Did you know ghee (in Indian food) is clarified butter or that soy sauce is high in salt? Everybody likes to eat with a man who knows his way round a menu so learn more about cooking styles and ingredients and what the dishes really contain.

Some menus give calorie and health information. If you're after the healthier options, avoid foods wrapped in pastry plus fried, battered or stuffed foods and go for grilled, baked or steamed dishes instead. Choose fish or a vegetarian option as a change and look out for buttery or creamy sauces.

Sharing desserts and starters is fun and means you get to try more stuff. Healthier too.

TWELVE TOP TIPS

Looking for simple pointers to healthier eating?

> Always have a **good breakfast** to start the day right.

> Eat mindfully. **Sit down and chew** each mouthful thoroughly and slowly.

> **Don't eat while distracted** by TV, phone surfing or reading.

> Choose healthy **snacks** between meals such as fresh fruit and unsalted nuts.

> **Plate smart**. Fill half your plate with salad or vegetables, one quarter with protein foods (eg lean meat, fish, eggs, beans) and one quarter with starchy carbohydrates (eg brown rice, wholewheat pasta, quinoa, baked potato, noodles).

> **Water** is usually the best rehydration fluid when exercising.

> Go easy on **alcohol** – it's particularly fattening.

> Smart **food substitutions** make healthy eating easy and painless.

> Keep a **food diary** - write down everything you eat and drink from the moment you wake until you go to bed. Accounting for everything that passes your lips helps you make healthier choices and reduce 'mindless' snacking.

> **Read labels**. Food nutrition labels help you make healthier choices such as cutting back on salt, sugar, and calories.

> If you choose lower fat, lower calorie or lower sugar versions of foods you eat regularly such as mayonnaise, salad dressings, yoghurt or milk, check labels carefully. Whatever is taken out is usually replaced with something else so low-sugar may be high-fat and low-fat may be high-sugar.

> **Enjoy** all the foods you like but in moderation. If they are full of fat or sugar, simply eat less of them and/or find some healthier options that taste just as good.

THE ONLY DIET THAT ALWAYS WORKS

Men often store fat around the waist where it is associated with higher blood pressure, cholesterol, diabetes and heart disease. But if you don't want a Diet with a capital D, what do you do?

First, assess the size of the problem. Find a tape measure and measure your waist. Measure around your middle at a point mid-way between the bottom of your ribs and the top of your hips (usually, this is the level of the belly button).

Men have a higher risk of health problems if their waist size is more than 94cm/37 inches. For Asian men, it's lower: 90cm/36 inches.

Trouser waistbands are not a good guide if your belly is hanging over the top (in which case a 36-inch waist might disguise a real measurement of 40+).

Just losing half a stone could significantly improve your health. And, contrary to popular belief, there is one diet that works every time:

> Prepare your normal meal and plate it up as usual.

> Remove half the food and place on another plate in the fridge or freezer for another day.

Easy enough? This approach cuts your cooking time, calorie intake and food expenditure in half. If it's still too much hassle, have two roast potatoes rather than four. Still too much hassle? Try the soup option from page 24.

It's about portion control. The amount you are currently eating alongside your current exercise levels has resulted in weight gain. Simple as that. You need to eat less and exercise more. This diet deals with the first bit in the easiest way.

WHATEVER YOU DO, TAKE EXERCISE

Whatever your life situation, maintain your level of exercise. Aim for 10,000 steps a day - 15,000 steps if you want to lose weight. A pedometer (or a fitness monitoring device or app) can help.